MOTEL OF THE
OPPOSABLE THUMBS

SOME OTHER BOOKS BY STUART ROSS

Espesantes (above/ground press, 2018)

The Dagmar Poems (w/ Michael Dennis; Burnt Wine Press, 2018)

Eleven/Elleve/Alive (w/ Dag T. Straumsvåg & Hugh Thomas; shreeking violet press, 2018)

Pockets (ECW Press, 2017)

A Sparrow Came Down Resplendent (Wolsak and Wynn, 2016)

Sonnets (w/ Richard Huttel; serif of nottingham editions, 2016)

A Hamburger in a Gallery (DC Books, 2015)

Further Confessions of a Small-Press Racketeer (Anvil Press, 2015)

In In My Dreams (Book*hug, 2014)

A Pretty Good Year (Nose in Book Publishing, 2014)

Nice Haircut, Fiddlehead (Puddles of Sky Press, 2014)

Our Days in Vaudeville (w/ 29 collaborators; Mansfield Press, 2013)

You Exist. Details Follow. (Anvil Press, 2012)

Snowball, Dragonfly, Jew (ECW Press, 2011)

I Have Come to Talk about Manners (Apt. 9 Press, 2010)

Buying Cigarettes for the Dog (Freehand Books, 2009)

Dead Cars in Managua (DC Books, 2008)

I Cut My Finger (Anvil Press, 2007)

Confessions of a Small-Press Racketeer (Anvil Press, 2005)

Hey, Crumbling Balcony! Poems New & Selected (ECW Press, 2003)

Razovsky at Peace (ECW Press, 2001)

Farmer Gloomy's New Hybrid (ECW Press, 1999)

Henry Kafka & Other Stories (The Mercury Press, 1997)

The Inspiration Cha-Cha (ECW Press, 1996)

The Mud Game (w/ Gary Barwin; The Mercury Press, 1995)

The Pig Sleeps (w/ Mark Laba; Contra Mundo Books, 1993)

He Counted His Fingers, He Counted His Toes (Proper Tales Press, 1979)

The Thing in Exile (w/ Steve Feldman & Mark Laba; Books by Kids, 1976)

MOTEL OF THE OPPOSABLE THUMBS

STUART ROSS

anvil
PRESS

Anvil Press Publishers Inc.
P.O. Box 3008, Station Terminal
Vancouver, BC V6B 3X5
www.anvilpress.com

Cover drawing: Stephen Lack
Cover design: Rayola.com
Interior design & typesetting: Stuart Ross

Library and Archives Canada Cataloguing in Publication

Title: Motel of opposable thumbs / Stuart Ross.

Names: Ross, Stuart, 1959- author.

Description: First edition. | Poems.

Identifiers: Canadiana 20190078189 | ISBN 9781772141269 (softcover)

Classification: LCC PS8585.O841 M67 2019 | DDC C811/.54—dc23

Printed and bound in Canada

Represented in Canada by Publishers Group Canada
Distributed in Canada by Raincoast Books; in the U.S. by Small Press Distribution (SPD)

The publisher gratefully acknowledges the financial assistance of the Canada Council for the Arts, the Canada Book Fund, and the Province of British Columbia through the B.C. Arts Council and the Book Publishing Tax Credit.

In memory of

Lily, 2009–2018
small dog, big love

Dave McFadden, 1940–2018
big life, small moments

Richard Huttel, 1954–2019
onward, brother!

CONTENTS

THE MOMENT OF MY DEATH

The Moment of My Death / 13

3 / 15

Efforts / 16

Behind the Supermarket / 17

The Phil Halls / 18

Bristles / 19

Alterations (Poem for January 1, 2016) / 20

Reading a Book with Jerry Lewis / 22

The North Star / 23

"Destiny" Doesn't Appear in This Poem's Title / 24

Poem Beginning with a Line by Dean Young / 27

Forty-Nine Cents / 28

This Is the Deck / 29

Toronto Poem / 30

Dream Analysis I / 31

Ken McGoogan, Age Two / 32

Threefold / 33

Motel Poem / 35

PLEASE WRITE THIS DOWN

Birthday / 41

My Question: A Cento / 42

Pencil Shavings / 43

Notley I / 45

Winter and Night / 46

Grey Snotes / 47

The Parents All Cried / 51

Poem Beginning with a Line by Kimiko Hahn / 52

Sunrise with Sea Monsters / 53

The Stapler's Staged Suicide / 54

Conniption Sauce / 55

The Option I Chose / 56

Expired Borscht / 57

Pro 5, Con 1: A Cento / 58

The Arrival of My Grandfather from Russia / 59

Please Write This Down / 60

YOU THREE WITH STONES UPON YOUR HEADS

Memory / 63

Picnic / 64

At Laundromats Here There Are No Dryers / 65

Broken Spoke / 66

George Bernard Shaw / 67

Me, in My Entirety / 68

Poetry or Baseball / 69

Fifty Words for Gwen, Plus a Title / 70

Poem Beginning with a Line by Sarah Manguso / 71

Rain / 72

You Step Out Onto Your Porch / 73

A Dog / 74

Retaliating with Yoko Ono / 75

Montreal Trilogy / 76

Occasional Poem / 78

Considerably Sarah / 79

Nancy / 80

Three Times / 82

Watching Sam and Dave with Nelson / 83

The Open Window / 84

Water / 85

You Three, with Stones Upon Your Heads / 86

The Road / 87

GOES WITHOUT SAYING

Guesswork / 91

From *The Poetics of Because* / 92

Movie / 93

Parc Avenue, August 11, 2018, 10:18 A.M. / 94

John Ashbery's "The Painter": Details / 96
24-Hour Cento / 97
Now Showing / 98
The Tragical History of the Life and Death of Dr. Walrus / 99
Suspicions / 100
The Schools Seem Pleased / 101
Mortality Cento / 102
Ladies & Gentlemen, the Solar System / 103
Important Information for Your Dental Health / 105
Static Is Terrible / 106
Goes Without Saying / 107
Incident Report / 108
Zigzag (Poem for January 1, 2017) / 109
Aphroditty / 110

WHATEVER YOU DESIRE

He: A Poetics / 113
The Food Court / 116
My Boss / 117
El Hindu / 118
The First Tetrapods / 119
Various Records (Poem for January 1, 2018) / 120
Ron Padgett's Poem "June 17, 1942" / 121
Love Is, Dot Dot Dot / 123
Poem Beginning with a Line by Dean Young / 124
Ironing / 125
Whatever You Desire / 126
Dream Analysis II / 127
Thrifty and Scaly / 128
Toronto / 129
Regarding My Greatest Work / 130
The Crowd / 131
Motel of the Opposable Thumbs / 133
Subtitles / 134
Notes on the Contributors / 137
Notes & Acknowledgements / 139

I see before me a bowl of grapes.
Now the grapes are gone.
I ate them all
but still it makes no sense.

—Larry Fagin, "Last Poem"

THE MOMENT OF MY DEATH

allegro

THE MOMENT OF MY DEATH

Ron Padgett and Charles North and Bill Berkson walk into a room.

Victor Coleman and Opal Louis Nations and Herman Neutics and Crad Kilodney walk into a room.

John Robert Colombo, I kid you not, walks into a room.

Larry Fagin walks into a room. It's Larry Fagin.

Nelson Ball and David W. McFadden and Diana Hartog and Robert Fones walk into a room.

Lisa Jarnot walks into a room, carrying a paperclip she loves.

Anne Waldman and Eileen Myles walk into a room.

George Miller walks into a room. So does Tom Clark.

Sarah Burgoyne walks into a room, with her saintly twin, Sarah Burgoyne.

Plus George Bowering. On Joe Rosenblatt's shoulders.

Also, have I mentioned yet, Daphne Marlatt. She walks into a room.

Tom Walmsley and D. M. Fraser walk into a room, plus bill bissett.

Heather Christle and Sommer Browning and Emily Pettit and Sawako Nakayasu, I do not know you, but you walk into a room.

bpNichol roams into a rune, a room.

Sam f. Johnson walks into a room with Paul Dutton, whom he does not know.

Bill Knott walks into a room, his glasses held together by tape. Richard Huttel enters a room, cradled in the arms of an ape.

Alice Burdick and Jaime Forsythe walk into a room. Plus Dag T. Straumsvåg, dragging a fjord.

John Lavery, he walks into a room. And Robin Wood.

Joe Brainard walks into a room, and Kenward Elmslie, a towel around his waist.

The record skips because there is dust on the stylus.

A light flickers across the page of a book.

The window blows open. A shout in the street.

3

I was going to write a poem about three things.

I forgot what they were.

I walked around in the kitchen, pacing in circles, opening and closing the cupboard doors, opening and closing the refrigerator door.

An ice cube fell out of the freezer and slid across the floor.

My dog ate it.

I am avoiding talking about something.

EFFORTS

I used the biggest words I could think of and spoke with an exaggerated Finnish accent. I cooked only foods requiring the most foul-smelling spices and watched only movies based on funeral processions. I smoked filterless cigarettes rolled by Guatemalan resistance fighters. I puffed out my chest and sucked in my ears. Have you ever had your fingers surgically transformed into suction cups and then walked across the ceiling of the Sistine Chapel? Do it all you want: see if she cares. It's true I don't know what a Finnish accent sounds like. I straighten my hair and I curl it. I lift several pounds above my head and breathe heavily. Finland is famous for its— Oh, I forgot what I was going to tell you. It is difficult to braid one's toes evenly. My heart is fulsome, like a successful harvest. She has, however, asked me to avoid similes. Do you know how many small dogs you can fit in a copy of *A Tree Grows in Brooklyn*? Do you know where I buried my lunch? Here is a fact about me: 1983 Finnish fencing champion with 20/20 vision. I squirted ketchup on an original Picasso. Or perhaps I tackled the man who squirted ketchup on an original Picasso. Choose whichever you prefer. I wear my glasses on my sleeve. Look! Now she is picnicking with the creatures of the forest.

BEHIND THE SUPERMARKET

You have asked me to pinpoint the location in which we
played gin rummy with a mongoose. This action took
place behind the supermarket. Also there: a wrestler*
printed hundred-dollar bills featuring the likeness of
Martin Heidegger. And I was left to sort out the various
emotions I felt:

> *anger*
>
> *despair*
>
> *glee*
>
> *porridge*
>
> *fortitude*
>
> *monkey wrench*. Behind the supermarket, I ate
a papier-mâché sparrow. Meanwhile, a plastic bag
crooned jazz standards and an onion plucked from your
eye† waited for a bus. Behind the supermarket, human
sacrifices were strictly prohibited. Famous people forgot
their own names. You handed me a bowling alley made
of refrigerators. The sun, behind the supermarket,
pondered whether to rise or set.

---

* Sweet Daddy Siki, karaoke DJ at the Duke.

† Plus rhubarb pie and steak. See Don Marquis.

THE PHIL HALLS

I hold out my hand. A tiny Phil Hall is in my palm. He holds a normal-size pencil, which to him, because he is tiny, is like a tree. He climbs the tree. Another tiny Phil Hall emerges from one of those creases in my palm. He starts sawing the tree. The first tiny Phil Hall tumbles into the air. The other one catches him. They kiss each other. I start walking down the street. Once so fond of each other, the two tiny Phil Halls are bickering about authorship. I say, "You taught me about threes, about putting things off-balance." In a record store, I set them free on the counter near the cash register. They begin racing toward the far end of the counter. One of them falls. The other stops, returns, and helps the first one back up to his feet. I buy a record by Screaming Females. I buy a record by the Grasping Straws. I buy a record by Siouxsie and the Banshees. The Phil Halls slip out the door when someone comes in. A woman wearing a toque approaches me. "My name is Clarice. Do you want to be in my band?" she asks me. "Yes," I reply. "We are called the Phil Halls," she states evenly. At our first show, we play only covers. When we are good enough, we will play only originals.

BRISTLES

for Dag T. Straumsvåg

Nestor couldn't get enough of shaving. He went through several blades each week. He had to excuse himself from conversations to shave. "It is because smoothness is so important to me," he told his friends, and later he told the television interviewers who clustered around him like bristles on a neglected chin. His girlfriend, Velda, was losing her patience. He often said, "Just a moment," several times during their lovemaking, and retreated to the bathroom to shave. At first she had thought he was just being considerate, but lately she had begun to develop another theory. Nestor's parents had grown up under a communist regime, where Nestor had spent his own first few years. Is it possible that each of the bristles on his chin reminded him of a different member of the Politburo and that Nestor, deeply affected as a child by his parents' irreversible melancholy, was obsessively battling the resurgence of communism by shaving the tyrants off his face? One morning, Velda tied Nestor's hands behind his back. His face felt calm. Then he began to struggle and wiggle about on the sofa. He strained and stretched his fingers and his arms. He rolled onto the floor. "My cuticles!" he shouted. "I need to push back my cuticles!" Velda got dressed and went to work. She was developing a new kind of escalator.

ALTERATIONS (Poem for January 1, 2016)

The weight of John Ashbery's
Collected French Translations:
Poetry (414 pages) and Roberto
Bolaño's *The Unknown University*
(835 pages) on my mattress this
New Year's morning is like
the weight of my mother and
father sitting on the foot of
the bed, watching me sleep.
Twenty-one years gone and fifteen,
respectively, they're from another
world. "What's a guy like you
doing here? / Are you plotting
a crime?" my father asks,
and he puts me in a headlock.
"O closed heart O heavy heart O
deep heart / You will never get
used to sorrow," my mother says,
and she strokes my left cheek.
Thing is, I've stopped writing
poems about them. Also,
my strides are longer, and
I can be out the door and
at the lake in three steps. I
kneel down and scoop
some water into my palm.
Soon the water turns to ice.
The weight of me makes me
sink into the snow that covers
the beach. By the time spring
comes and the snow has melted,
I will have a little tailor shop
down there. I will have become
my grandfathers. My parents

are just a gleam in my eye.
I switch a tiny light on
above my sewing machine
and do some alterations.

READING A BOOK WITH JERRY LEWIS

A wall falls off my house
and people walking by can
see into every room, like
the room where Jerry Lewis
and I are reading a
collection of stories by
Isaac Bashevis Singer. Jerry
got it from the library. I
don't use the library because
I am frightened of bedbugs—
like my friend Kim in Manhattan,
she once got them and had
to put all her books on the
roof in winter. I have to
be in bed by 8 o'clock
unless there is a Jerry
Lewis movie on. Jerry
exists outside of the laws
of gravity and the laws
of time. I pull on my boots,
shovel the driveway, and
make stupid sounds.

THE NORTH STAR

for Laurie Siblock

The first time I meet Laurie I walk into her house and hand her a jar of pickles. Her father's side of the family is Ukrainian, and therefore she loves pickles, she must love pickles, I have brought her some pickles. I hand her two roses, each rose is orange, one for her and its echo for her cat, who has recently died, a rose for each. In the park near the beach, she wraps her arms around a tree too thick for her to wrap her two arms around. Her smile is composed of her eyes, her cheeks, her lips, her teeth, her nose, the depths of her, the air that surrounds her. Across the lake is Rochester, you'll find Rochester there, where Frederick Douglass launched the *North Star*, his abolitionist newspaper, in eighteen hundred and forty-seven.

"DESTINY" DOESN'T APPEAR IN THIS POEM'S TITLE

And you, you come down from the sky,
and the committee meets to define the word "sky"—
bird-holder, cloud-bearer, cradler of airplanes,
referee between earth and oblivion.
Of the airplanes, and those within them:
see their noses pressed to the windows,
their breath creates fog, their fingers manipulate
plastic water cups, their luggage gasps
in the chamber below them. And I, I hit
only bloopers. My baseball sails above my neighbours'
lawns, wobbling in mid-air, smacking gnats
off their gnat-paths, singing a song it once heard
about peanuts and home runs, and a postman
with limbs so long and skinny he looks
like a water strider, and had his name
legally changed to Water Bug, he reaches up
and catches the slow-motion ball, and
at that moment you slide into a taxi
and hurtle into a city you have never seen.
The driver turns around and hands you a list
of the things the city contains: chickens,
for starters, plus ray guns and chess sets,
records by Nana Mouskouri, fiddleheads,
postage stamps, Crock-Pots, a biography
of the Quintuplet Twins, and several
barrels of carpet vaccine. And I, I sit in
the centre of a quivering field of weeds,
thunderstruck and shadowstruck and soothing
my wounds with poultices made of corpulent
snapdragons. Soon we will meet at
the place we agreed on in a dream
you don't remember. I want to look good.
I want to look at least as good as my shadow.

My shadow contains three words:
Sh. Ad. Ow. I contain multitudes
of headlice I'm hoping to comb out
before you arrive with your eyes in your face,
your hair hanging down from your oval head.
And now, as your driver pulls over for a smoke,
you repose in the stream of words,
absorbing the language of this new place
so you can make people here understand you.
Let me tell you about myself. I spent
my formative years looking for three
of my heads. I had misunderstood when my mother
said, "Let me feel your forehead." Four?
I felt only one when I reached up
to prod above my neck. After I was formed,
which took several years of sleep and toil,
I crawled from the foot of Bathurst Street
to the wiggling boundary of Steeles Avenue, chalking in
a hopscotch court in front of every lemonade
stand. International conflicts were resolved
in these courts. I had a cup of tea in a smoke-filled
doughnut shop. The name of the shop was
Round With A Whole In The Middle, which
I thought was very clever. Do you?
And by you, I mean you who have just arrived
and absorbed the locals' language, plus watched
bug-eyed as the concrete splendour of this new
city unfolded to pull the warmth of you
into its cold and noisy arms. Soon we will
meet in the place we agreed on in a dream
you've confused with a best-selling novel.
You are concerned about readership. You touch
the tip of your right index finger to the tip

of your tongue and engage in moisture transfer.
You use this damp fingertip to turn the page
of your eyelids down, and you disappear into
a sleep that features birds falling from the sky
and landing on mirrors forged of cotton phenomena.
Look how they stretch and yawn and coo. They
know I have written this poem and they
turn to me and say, "It might not look like it now
but someday you will make something of yourself
and someone will carry you somewhere where
somehow you will realize that not only has it
already started but it's already practically finished."
I think they're talking about my life. I pat my pockets
but all they contain is a crumpled Polaroid of you
and a pass for a miniature golf course
in the Pannahill Road of my tottering head.

POEM BEGINNING WITH A LINE BY DEAN YOUNG

Behind you a whisper, in front a windy blur.
A coyote appears at your side.
You raise your arms in the air.
Beneath the ground,
worms emulate you,
raising their arms in the dirt.
Worms don't have arms.
Coyotes don't have segments.
But they are agreeable
companions, who always
lend you money or love.
Air murmurs between your fingers.

FORTY-NINE CENTS

for Steve Venright

A quick survey of the wreckage indicates that a Norwegian Forest cat was piloting the plane, having taken over the controls when Captain Whisper became engrossed in a short early novel by Roberto Bolaño (1953–2003) shortly after takeoff from Trondheim Airport, Værnes. The weather was unremarkable. Shards of the port wing tip and the plane's nose were discovered off the Chilean island Desventuradas, home to ten species of seabirds and one land bird, discovered by Juan Fernández on November 6, 1574 (the island, not the land bird). The cat, the flight's sole survivor, declined to give interviews to Televisión Nacional. When I was a child, a man approached me in the Coles bookstore in Yorkdale Mall and offered to buy me a collection óf Andy Capp comics, created by British cartoonist Reg Smythe (1917–1998). I thanked him and declined. Thirty minutes later, in Kresges department store, I bought my mother a blue brooch for forty-nine cents. In 1970, forty-nine cents was equivalent to three dollars and seven cents in today's currency. She told me the man in the bookstore was planning to kidnap me. Not long before my mother died, she said the blue brooch was her most treasured piece of jewellery. Not being kidnapped sure was a relief.

THIS IS THE DECK

for Kennedy Enns

I knew there was something I had to do
and sticking a deck on the side of my house
was that thing. A deck is a horizontal surface
incorporating wood and nails. These are things
you can do on the deck that is stuck
on the side of your house: you can stand
on it, plus barbecue dead animals, play board
games like Lemur In The Family! and
also Punch The Car. You can jog, sing,
and age. The possibilities are limited
only by your imagination. My deck keeps
falling off but I tell my neighbours
it's on purpose. They watch with binoculars
from their decks. If you really listen
to your deck, you can become very
interesting.

TORONTO POEM

Toronto, the taxi cabs flow mournfully
through your hunchbacked streets. Anxious
towers reach into the white-haired clouds
that throw shadows over
your tired, sweaty people, who squeeze
between each other on self-conscious
sidewalks cracking open beneath the
weight of fearful commerce and
vanishing newspapers. Your edges ripple
and fade into devoted car-worshipers.
Your tired mechanics and surgeons
work deep into the noisy night,
Jewish poodles sniffing at
their inquisitive ankles.

DREAM ANALYSIS I

I was on Coxwell,
near Gerrard. Kevin
was there too. He
was putting up posters
with a stapler. The
posters were solid
red. I asked Kevin
what the posters
were for. He said,
"They are for my
new reading series,
The Red Revolver."
This was a dream.

In dreams, staplers represent the need to talk, and posters are the flesh that covers our bones and muscles. I need to talk with my flesh. In dreams, Kevin represents hope and success, whereas I represent illness and death. I hope to successfully die. In dreams, revolvers represent fungal infections, and red means hunger. Disease can feed the world. In this way, I solve both personal and universal crises while resting my body and mind.

KEN McGOOGAN, AGE TWO

for Kate Sutherland

Ken McGoogan, age two,
is the author of several
legitimate books
about science and entertainment.
His father, Dundee Saskatoon,
is closer to the surface,
his face pressed against the ice,
his wrists shackled
though in truth he died
of a punch to the gut
by Harry Houdini. I don't know
if I'm making this up.
The quadruped you saw in
Scott's ship (first
expedition) wrote a monograph
about selling pieces
of the original ship
at an exhibition
in the original ship
which sits in the lap
of Lady Scott
who sits in the
original ship. I don't
know if I am making
this up. I, age two,
the author of a
monograph about
the role of the Venus
flytrap in U-boat
detection during
World War I'm
not sure which.

THREEFOLD

i

I ran down to the beach and I ran around on the beach. The beach was covered in snow. My feet kicked up the snow when I ran. I threw myself down onto the beach and pressed my face in the snow. The lake tried to eat me. I screamed into the snow and snow got in my mouth. I plunged my fingers into the world and held on. The world was moving so fast I couldn't find my breath. I heard my voice sail into the sky and disappear behind the thick clouds. My fingers got tired from holding on. I was thrown somewhere and when I woke, I looked around. I didn't see anything made of anything I recognized.

ii

I am distracted for a moment by a cloud's sudden movement. Meanwhile, the horizon gathers in the distance and comes rolling toward me over the fields. Hearing its roar, I wheel around to see it. I turn and run, but now the other horizon has bunched like a giant shoulder and barrels toward me too, skipping over small lakes and streams. Everywhere I look: the horizon, unstoppable. The ground tugs me to it where I stand and soon I am kneeling and throw my arms around my spinning head. I press my eyes shut, cover my ears, but there it is: the angry bellow of the ends of the earth.

iii

I will reach my arms out and stretch them. They will go for miles. Eventually, my arms will wrap around the horizons and down the sides of the earth and across the bottom. They will wrap until my hands meet. It has been so long since they have seen each other. Months, or maybe years. With my remaining energy, I will squeeze the earth. It will get increasingly compact until it is a tiny pebble sitting on my chest. I will realize I am alone. I can't get in. My friends will be in there, and my books, and my dog. My grandfather's tefillin will be in there. This little pebble rocking on my chest, it will hold everything I've loved. I will let it tumble into the palm of my hand. I will stare at it, try to stare into it. I will see nothing. I will fling it into that which had surrounded it. Let it sail where it needs to. Watch it go.

MOTEL POEM

after Charles Henri Ford

*In my last letter, I wrote of my journey across Canada during the Thirteenth
World War. Herein follows a list of the motels at which I took the opportunity
to rest my ravaged body.*

Motel More Sleep
Motel Thunderbolt
The Fallacy Motel
Motel Sans Temps
Motel How Do You Do?
Curved Spine Inn
Motelevision
Motel Piece of Cake
Joe Rosenblatt Miracle Motel
Motel Motel Motel!
Motel Sleep Not War
Motel Give Me Some
Motel of Facile Idealism
Do-Me-In Inn
El Motel Sin Embargo
Motel Baudelaire
Motel of Hungry Bankers
Motelekinetics
Motel of Surgery Gone Wrong
Put Up Your Feet Motel
There Their They're Motel
Motel La Soeur de Carole Laure
Motel of Pompous Conceits
Motel Limbless
Motel Made-of-Bricks
Motelian Stallion
Motel Suspension of Mercy
Stone Angel Inn

Edible Woman Inn

Canadian Healing Oil Motel

Motel Watch Your Step

Sleep Inn

Fit Right Inn

Motel of the Unconscious Narrative

Motel of Minor Errors

Shave-Rite Motel

Motel Have-a-Pee

Elegant Bedbug Roadside Inn

Motel Spelunk More

Forn-U-Cate Inn

Motel Mat O'Door

Motel Sitting Shiva

Motel de Rien

Motelosaurus Rest

Motel Short End of the Stick

Motel Burning at Both Ends

Feel Good Motel

Motel Désastre

All Cartoon Favourites Inn

A Higher Motelligence

Clean Motel

Motel Antipsychiatrie

Happy Accident Motel

Motel Short Back and Sides

Motel Can You Feel the Magic

Motel of the Soft White Pillows

GeSTOPo for the Night Inn

Motel of the Five Canadas

Motel Sand-Inn-ista

Who's Inn Charge

Motel of the Uncertain Narrative

Florence Night-in-Gale Motel

Motel of the Thousand Fan Dances

Affordable Inn

Motel My Word!
Adequate Motel
Honeymoon Bliss Motel
Elton Motel-lo
Motel of the Weeping Virgin
Motel of the Unfinished Sestina
Jump Right Inn
Friendly to Pets Motel
Motel Three-Sixty
Off-Chance Motel
Motel No Second Chance
Motel Artful Rendezvous
Motel of Careful Pronunciation
Motel Tabernacle
Motel Can You Hear the Owl's Cry?
Motel Cloud François
Motel Splendid Vista Don't You Think?
Brother Antoninus Roadside Inn
Motel Chambres Amoreux
Not Abandoned Motel
Motel of the Short Reign of Kim Campbell
Posthumous Motel
Malicious Hacker Inn
Motel Objection Sustained
Mainstream Poetry Motel
Motel Drop Wrist
By the Way Inn
Motel Spotted Deer
Motel I Heart Slovenia
Luckily Seven Motel
Motel of the Opposable Thumbs
In Crowd Inn
Motel You Leave Me No Choice

Esteemed reader, none of these distinguished motels have paid me a single goddamn penny to include them in my poem. For god's sake look after our people.

PLEASE WRITE THIS DOWN

prestissimo, con sordino

BIRTHDAY

A pigeon stared down at me.
I denied myself everything
(because it was my birthday).
But in the cave of tattoos
all they could offer was
a terrible kind of pleasure.
The air-raid siren banged my head.
A squirrel plunged its teeth in my ankle.
While I washed my shattered dishes
I saw them through the window:
they talked deep into the quivering night.
When he hung up the phone
she hid all her philosophy books
under the mouldy sofa bed.
In the diner destroyed by fire
he ordered a tuna sandwich
with a pair of pliers
torn out of his head
like a piece of wood and a river.

MY QUESTION: A CENTO

I am listening to a life
short and fat, thick-necked.
I shall root for Tom.
He salutes the steaming horse dung
because a month before he died
he ran and banged his head
at incredible speed, traveling day and night
around the outdoor rink my parents poured
in honor of my beloved mother.
My sister insisted on rescuing ladybugs.
She drowned her nakedness,
melting the billowing snow with wine.
But in the small university classroom
there are people so sick
I suck on the pit of my question.

PENCIL SHAVINGS

I

I kept one eye on myself
and one eye on the wall behind me.
My other eye I devoted
to my profound zest for life
as the horse beneath me
took off, and it occurred
to every ship on the horizon
that the sky is parallel
to the highway. Each object
in the palms of our hands
has a particular meaning.
They mean we have noses:
those of us, in authority,
who have noses. Beloved,
I want to single you out,
berate you, because
I am sincere, I am decent,
I am conflated with
the barn in which I was born,
named, educated, pummelled,
and decorated with medals
that sparkle like some
kind of fish made of
pencil shavings.

II

And now, I must
cradle my nerves, erupting
inside the convenient box,
sniffing out my father's
anger. What did you say
was abandoned? And what
was left over? Cake? An airplane?
A handshake? The way
we got born and thus were forced
to exist, like pastry and
raccoons, it was like making
hay on a pink beach. When
we become old, after so much
wine and so many shouting
insects, we gaze into the stars,
newsprint straining our eyes,
scurrying between A and B,
until the streetscape shares
with us its freshly
unwrapped secrets.

NOTLEY 1

Something. Especially an amount of money, donated. His love poems, religious poems, satires, elegies, and sermons. A person who predicts disaster, especially of American rhythm and blues groups of the 1950s, in which nonsense southeast of Rotterdam, population 114,152. Situated on one of any of various marine fish having a compressed bend or curl up. Cause to do this, especially by a blow. Be overcome practising deceit, arms or legs to bend backwards as well as forwards, a twofold blow or setback introducing innovative social reforms such as hospital insurance; he led with a dowel or dowels. Names of race tracks, the intended target, away from the launching pad and along the downward deflection of an English novelist and editor. Her clothes usually worn by the opposite sex, dry by providing an outflow for moisture. Carry off the repertoire, etc., for game. Make by pulling a piece of metal through a string that can be pulled to tighten the mouth garbage; worthless junk. A person or thing with shelves above for displaying plates, etc., following a mineral vein. A large mass of especially flowering plants form idiotically run at the mouth or nose. Dribble that runs or proceeds in a certain way. Fall asleep. Leave or deposit something at a crowd, a multitude, a shoal, a great number combining traditional Inuit dancing with Scottish and French-Canadian, having little or no aftertaste, due to longer brewing, without acid. An engraving produced with this Jamaican vernacular, originally accompanied by dub music fried to acquire a crisp surface.

WINTER AND NIGHT

from the novel by S. J. Rozan

That menace nodded.
Guns think.
Have you thought?
Two boys was alone.
Her voice like that diner.
A five pushed the door
into the cold.
A cigarette cupped my hands,
pulled the phone from
my pocket. You're big and free.
I want big.
Unless you bust you.
Just meaning. The end.

GREY SNOTES

for Nicholas Power

a French word
spilled off the table
and into
the faceless ocean

&

I kept a record
of how many breaths
my mother took
before the rain
carried her voice
into my sleep

&

a task completed
is a task completed
to the forest's
moist satisfaction

&

she looked up and down
the row of empty lockers
and a bowling ball
hurtled past her feet
with something urgent
to tell the president

&

one of the turnstiles
from Montmorency station
turned up
in my salad

&

ovation:
the egg stood up
for itself

&

the fastest way to
wreck a perfectly
good poem is
to mention a jazz
musician—watch:
Lionel Hampton

&

all the kids
laughed at me
because I wore my
shorts upside down

&

give the restless gibbon
a first-place ribbon
and some good-natured ribbin'

&

keep on truckin'
Gabe Gudding's poetry
over the border
in unmarked
bowling bags

&

I held my Etch-A-Sketch
over my head
and shook it hard.
When I put it back down
it was still an Etch-A-Sketch
but it had replaced Elizabeth Taylor
in *A Place in the Sun*.

&

Larry Fagin told me to
write boring endings
on my poems.
Boiled lamb.

&

Today only:
Plabo
Pissaco.

&

if you double a bubble
you will have two bubbles
but this information isn't worth
a pile of rubble

&

rabbits have one head
(each)
not two
as you recently
stated

&

the wedding
knocked the chuppah
right out of me

&

a painting of
a woolly mammoth
husked corn
at the county fair
while waiting for the results
of the macaroni art
competition

THE PARENTS ALL CRIED

It was a quiet time for us.
A man with two heads lived in our garage.
The price of fuel was plummeting.
Mother had already collected
twenty miniature folksingers.
We hid beneath our desks
because a crow had gotten in.
Outside, a jalopy was idling.
The lights went out when
Velda, the janitor,
slammed the classroom door.
Our teacher's voice was soothing.
We lay on the floor on mats.
The radios began sputtering;
the televisions went black.
In St. Petersburg, explosions were heard.
We lifted our Barbies and Kens
and chewed the heads off our dolls.
The parents all cried
when the monkey bars fell. We
took the broken tricycle and
flung it into the canyon.

POEM BEGINNING WITH A LINE BY KIMIKO HAHN

She became a sink.
She painted a black line
around herself
on the wall
behind herself.
At night,
she snuck into
an art gallery,
dragging the wall
with her.
A man with a moustache
shot a bicycle.
Everyone in the escalator
was naked.
I adjust.

SUNRISE WITH SEA MONSTERS

A horse sat down
on the bench beside me.

"Look at the bunny," it said,
"leaping into the sun."

Water is very popular. You can see through it. A horse and I noticed it in the distance. We couldn't get enough of that fluid. It constituted much of us. We became unusually thirsty. When we tried to hang the water on our living room wall, it tumbled to the floor. There it did roil. Aye, it roiled.

THE STAPLER'S STAGED SUICIDE

They lifted me beneath the armpits
and threw me bodily
into the conference room
The president was sneezing and
the treasurer danced poorly
near the water cooler
I pulled out my hair until
the man holding the earwigs flinched
and growled through his teeth
"It is not true that I
spit in your grandfather's eye"
We glanced at each other
Before the coffee was ready
someone's unleashed cocker spaniel
pounced on my grammatical error
When the window blew open
the entire committee shrieked
because I closed my eyes
held my breath
and pushed the stapler
off the edge of the desk

CONNIPTION SAUCE

after John Ashbery

I am enthralled
as I sink, nose first,
into a daily miracle
on the side of a
confused hill over which teem
a corridor of tender knives.
I am the inventor of
conniption sauce. The costume
I wear is that of my
worst enemy peering into
a billowing funhouse mirror.
Did it ever occur to you
that you were born into a
wet barn on a cruise ship?
I don't know if it's
even true, but it's a fact.
My teeth clench my heart.
Do yours? I'm sorry:
I gave you the slip
on the edge of
whatever happens to be
Main Street. A number
of gargoyles still love you,
even though you are so-so.

THE OPTION I CHOSE

The extinction fan club
was slow to exhume the remains
of a cloud repeated like
wallpaper across the sky.
My balloon red, I was happy
to follow the exact bend in the road,
soon reaching a serenade of flaming cars.
In my pocket: a conductor, an almond, and a rubber band.
The option I chose was the plastic ship,
which I placed into a puddle and climbed aboard.

EXPIRED BORSCHT

for Terry Taylor, and for Linda and Ted Crosfield

Borscht is circular
when viewed from above.
Both hot borscht and
cold are in fashion.
Also, there is a wedding
recipe and a funeral one.
The sticker says before
May 21 but it's May 22.
There are 40,000 Doukhobors
in Canada. Each one is
shaped differently. "Doukhobor"
means "snowflake" in Ukrainian.
If you eat expired borscht,
several untoward things occur.
I will list them in my next
book. Part of a Doukhobor
village has been preserved
in Grand Forks, British
Columbia. "Doukhobor"
does not mean "snowflake"
in Ukrainian. In 1944, seven
Doukhobors went on a hunger
strike near Nelson, B.C.
Depending on how expired
the borscht is, you might need
the funeral version.

PRO 5, CON 1: A CENTO

You stare and do not blink
You want my belly for good
You won't enjoy the shoving and pushing
You can't force people to take an interest

We are spaghetti
We are all holy
We call it light
We were drunk

Who would read a book by a Western Samoan
Who could have imagined it?
Whose tongues are ruby arrows
Who wears my fur, who dwells in my shell

I know where we have been
I know the road kill
I don't have to listen to you
I see no solution

She lost her voice from cigars
She used to appear in my office completely naked
She is never lost in sleep
She could not die

and when your voice ascends the air
and how the bare feet knead the wet grass
and men were praised for fighting in alleys
And where is the suffering in that?

THE ARRIVAL OF MY GRANDFATHER
FROM RUSSIA

after Louise Glück

A big memory fell on my head
while I was living in the adventurous
lighthouse. My head was bright
and in it I lay awake,
buzzing. You ask what kind of
pyjamas I wore. My pyjamas
were made of silver paper.
My grandfather was by then
a puffy cloud bearing
two children across the sky.
The sky lay between the yellowing,
clenched teeth of a sudden
dog, who flung it repeatedly
into the air. I replaced
my voice with that of
my grandfather. I found this
very shocking. Footsteps.

PLEASE WRITE THIS DOWN

after Barbara Guest

An egg gallops. It wears a ring, splashes into a pool of
tangled syllables. The head of a sparrow replaces my
own head, so we'll have enough time to share a marble
tomato and dance among the nubile chairs of elsewhere.

Have you ever been lost in a forest? Have you ever
escaped from a thieving potato field? Feel the brush
of leaves across your brow, something cold across your
dark and dignified throat. Have you ever used the
word "apparatus" in a poem? I just did. And thus the
poem smells.

Crawl into this careless, embittered bed, and gaze at
the wall opposite, where a photograph is mounted of
the president of Switzerland, pens hanging out of his
nostrils. Little did we know that we would someday
fling our watches—and our wrists—from the pebble-
strewn road.

Please write this down. Write this down while giving
me a look both contaminated and affectionate. All by
yourself, you have invented the laboratory.

YOU THREE WITH STONES
UPON YOUR HEADS

non troppo lento

MEMORY

I can't
remember

the last time
I wrote
a short
story. Oh

yes I can.
One
minute ago.

PICNIC

Laurie
spreads
a blanket,
places
a bag
of samosas
on it, a
dried
sausage
stick.
The samosas
are for us.
Lily gets
her first
taste
of sausage.

It is dusk.
Black birds
perforate
the darkening
sky
above
the lake.
We pluck
bits of
grass
from
Lily's
fur. She
barely
notices.

AT LAUNDROMATS HERE THERE ARE NO DRYERS

Where I am, bicycles have no wheels.
Figs have no trees. The protests
in the streets have no protestors.
The garbage bins are lidless.

Firecrackers, incidentally,
have no wicks. Rats have no
hammocks, and fish aren't able
to read. Do you see, now,
how different it is here?

My clothes are soaked
but they are clean. I pull them on
and walk through the park
where the temperature has
no limit. I lie back in the grass
that has no ants, peer
into the sky that has no birds.

But the clouds here, I haven't
yet mentioned the clouds here:
they sing these very personal songs
about wronging and being
wronged. They smoke a lot
of cigarettes. You can hear it.
And I sing along though I have
no voice. I sing with my eyes.

BROKEN SPOKE

after Mary Ruefle

Everything gets smaller.
The world glows.
You grow an extra arm.
Fluttering from branches
the sewer backs up.
Forehead of Gorbachev:
This is peace.
When the sun explodes
you have completed your task.

*

A shadow covers your mouth.
There is so much of you.
You are this,
torn from oak trees.
The sun evades you.
Wizened hand clutching a—
We are that.
Fog gulps you whole.
A clothesline swings from your balcony.

*

Vines grow out of your ears.
Everybody sings to you.
But you don't forgive yourself
hanging precariously from dead branches.
An ant is carried, too, by the breeze
with the hand of a grandmother who fries chicken fat.
Red denotes embarrassment.
When the moon is hurled behind clouds,
you are filled with acceptance.

GEORGE BERNARD SHAW

A cat hangs from the chandelier
from the chandelier, a letter arrives
a letter arrives outlining my death
my death will occur in nineteen stages
nineteen stages can accommodate nineteen plays
nineteen plays are too much for a single playwright
a single playwright puts a personal ad in the paper
the paper tells me the president has died
the president has died in one stage
one stage of grief is laughter
"grief is laughter" said George Bernard Shaw
George Bernard Shaw had a cat.

ME, IN MY ENTIRETY

I am not
a vendor of cacti
shivering in the rancid snow.

I am not
part of a conspiracy
to wrest the championship
from the ugly Russians.

I am not
prepared to answer the phone
upon which you
smeared your feces.

I am not
expecting company
in my cell on death row.

I am not
pushing this stroller,
filled with dirt and worms,
along the damp boulevard.

I am not
going to take responsibility
for your actions
or your word choices.

POETRY OR BASEBALL

From the kayak
I see George turn to Jean,
his lips move, hands swing
in air—because he is
Bowering it's poetry or baseball
or the story of Audie
Murphy. I feel safe only
when the kayak is moving.
Now it is still,
like Slocan Lake. I grasp
the craft's edges
to steady my nerves
and feel the sun
punish the back
of my neck. I pull
the oar and push through
the water toward the small
sandy beach where
the glacier flattened
the earth
and there I arrived,
alive and unbowed.
George and Jean
were specks now,
they were just specks
across Slocan Lake,
or they may have been sun spots
or Leo Gorcey.

FIFTY WORDS FOR GWEN, PLUS A TITLE

Every day something magical
happens. Every day is a day
to do everything. You can
do up to and more than fifty things
every day. Or none. There are
no rules. A dandelion
goes surfing. A sewing machine
wins the Nobel Peace Prize.
You count to fifty.
And look! Magic!

POEM BEGINNING WITH A LINE BY SARAH MANGUSO

I'm walking through the metal detector.
Grief is a lead ball in my gut.
I find myself imprisoned.
Will I get two or four hours in the exercise yard?
Will I ever see a Jerry Lewis movie again?
Will my mother know what's become of me?
My mother is twenty-two years' dead.
We still talk on the phone, though.
Remember the time I fell on a nail?
She made me better.
My cellmate borrows my eyelids.
I'm glad to help him sleep.

RAIN

for Nelson Ball

The sky
starts to blister

We scamper
every
which way

gather the
dented
buckets

Thump
thump

Beating
hearts
and various
other
organs.

YOU STEP OUT ONTO YOUR PORCH

for Michael Dennis

You step out onto your porch
and there is a cat in your garden.
You pour a glass of wine for yourself,
another for the cat.
A kid whips by on a skateboard.
A star arcs across the dark sky.

Inside your house, paintings and
sculptures crawl up and down the walls,
rearrange themselves and await
your return. When they do this,
they think you don't notice
but you do, every time. Meanwhile,
Laura Nyro does guest vocals
on a Miles CD, and your
Buk books secretly read
bpNichol. Kirsty is finally
rewarded with sainthood,

and you finish your wine,
then drink the cat's.
After all, you have written seventeen
poems today. You deserve it.

A DOG

A dog broke in half
and half of him fell in the water
and half in the arms of God.

A dog broke in half
and we put her together
again wrong.

A dog broke in half
and each of the halves
ran in opposite directions,
found different
owners.

A dog broke in half
because she couldn't hear
the crickets' chirping
or the slap of the paper
hitting the door.
She couldn't hear
her water bowl empty.

A dog found his tail
on the rear of another dog
and followed that dog
everywhere
until one of them died.

RETALIATING WITH YOKO ONO

My neighbour is playing
some awful folk, like

Steeleye Span, something
horrible. My heart pounds.

I break open my
Yoko Ono Box Set,

sealed now for 17 years,
and blast it through the

ceiling. I pour my tea and wait.

MONTREAL TRILOGY

There is an apple in my hand.
I brung it from that store over there.
Without it my hand would be empty
and you could see the lines in my palm
that say I will lead a life
of many ups and downs
and one time a guy in the street
(he's got a torn T-shirt that says
You Light Up My Life with a cartoon
picture of a firefly wearing a top hat)
will ask me if I have money for food
and I will present my hand
and within it shall dwell an apple.

*

They got a bridge table on their lawn.
It's covered in ashtrays and beer bottles.
At night when I walk by I hear them
around it, their laughter, voices. I see
hovering glows of cigarette tips but
I do not see them. There's dark smudges
which I don't know if it's them or just
a bunch of bushes or maybe raccoons.
Their lives aren't perfect, like it
looks like. When it's daytime
they have problems.

*

Here all the bars close at three a.m.
Everyone's holding a slice of wilted
pizza. Their shoes skid on the sidewalk
on other people's vomit. Look! A new
ice cream shop just opened (literally
just now) beside the store displaying
electric shavers and hand-held fans
in the window. In one hour
they will have been open for a whole
hour, and the hands of the people
on the sidewalk become filled with
cones of vanilla and pistachio almond.
It's like this is a whole new street
that some rich guy just built.

OCCASIONAL POEM

after Larry Fagin

Mark Laba and I took the Yonge
subway downtown because we wanted
to eat lunch in Chinatown. Mark
pretended to have a wooden leg to
make the woman beside us uncomfortable.
(I don't know if she was; maybe *she*
had a wooden leg.) At Bloor station,
people really poured on. It was so
crowded that we were squished against
each other. At Dundas we poured
out and Mark and I went to Kwong
Chow's where we had the 85-cent lunch
special: fried rice, chicken balls, chow
mein, and consomée soup. We were 15
years old. After we read our fortune
cookies—Mark's said "You are a well-
respected man"—we went to Village Bookstore
where Marty sold us some poetry books
from New Directions. Back on the subway,
Mark said he liked to drink pickle juice
and when I saw him the next week
he did exactly that.

CONSIDERABLY SARAH

The spoon is small. I step into it and slide about in its concavity. I am filling with spoon dreams. A typewriter is balanced on my knees, it suddenly notices. I offer you invisible gifts, so many that they spill out of your arms, arms made entirely of prepositions. Your friends salute you. The sun, wriggling around in the red sky, is only a small dog. Such a small dog with so many eyebrows. One hundred and seven people squeeze into your living room. Your open hand has been open so long. I walk you across the street (we each use our own feet). We look up and beckon the sky. You direct a movie in which the eclipsed sun gathers its radiance into a seven-haloed choir: this is the exact hour when the ship comes in. The credits come rolling down the hills. The fishes laugh and set out the saucers. A constant state of thought shuffles through the fields. You are the you who creates the old books. Hello!

— 30 —

NANCY

in memory of Joe Brainard

It's time for your bath, baby—
Did you **really** get this right from a cow?
I sold one to Mr. Jones on Elm Street this morning—
I've sure got smart brains.

Are you goofy?
The first thing we'll do is
go to a hotel and rent some rooms.
It don't get enough sunshine down here.

How **dare** you hang your coat
on the light fixture? Don't get
the table legs wet! **Oh, yeah?**
My ball is stuck in the mouth of your bear rug.

How do you stand the insects around here?
I don't feel anything. Gangway!
Suppose you take my muff—
If you don't...I'll leave you.

Gandhi. Wow! What a mustache.
I can't quite hear you.
Abba dabba zinga bix—
Now yer talkin'...let's start walkin'.

I wish I was that bird...
I wish we had a maid...
I'd love to be a duck or rabbit...
Plato called me an orchid!

You can untie my hands, now!
You said I could direct traffic today!
Have you seen the tube of toothpaste?
You can make some toast while I go up and wash.

A few weeks ago it fell off
the window ledge. Will you
lend me a nickel? I can't find one.
I just cleaned up the museum floor.

You just declared war on
the Zabooga tribe. I thought
you were working at the drug store.
I had quite a shock.

I wonder what Nancy is up to.
It must be awful to be so lonely.
Go to your meeting, Nancy!
Mmff...fnnf...fmmx...

THREE TIMES

At midnight,
I take Lily out
for a last
pee. She pees.
Then walks a little
further, sits
in the grass.
I sit beside her.
We get up, take
a few more steps
toward our porch.
Lily sits in the grass.
I sit beside her.
We get up, take
a few more steps.
Lily sits in the grass.
I sit beside her.
She lies down
and I place my hand
on her soft, firm
belly, riding
her breaths
up and down.

WATCHING SAM AND DAVE
WITH NELSON

"Did you see
Donald
'Duck'
Dunn laugh

at something

Dave said?
I wonder

what he said."
I can't believe

I'm watching
music videos

with Nelson
Ball.

THE OPEN WINDOW

What Ingvild told me turned out to be true.
The buildings were shifting,
gliding slowly over the concrete.
And the people were drifting too,
even that guy just standing there
reading the newspaper. The river
had already moved twelve metres,
and the ravine, plus our favourite
bar, Yammy the Cat. Remember
the night we spent there, writing
poems while the bartender
slumped over the counter, asleep?
Above the streets, the bats were sliding
through clouds; they flapped
one way but they headed another.
The clouds skidded across
the grey sky, and the words
drifted from the pages we read.
I asked Ingvild how long
this would last, but her answer
wafted into an open window.
When I leaned forward
to kiss her hair,
it sailed toward the old
bus station. I bought
a ticket but it slipped
from my fingers and crept
along the sidewalk.
On my hands and knees
I watched the moon
drop beneath the horizon
and I tried to stop
the earth's rotations.

WATER

Lily
drinks
so
much
water
now.
I
gently
squeeze
it
from
her
sopping
chin
and,
with
a
single
fingertip,
trace
it
down
her
lush
back,
where
her
honey
streak
has
turned
black.

YOU THREE, WITH STONES UPON YOUR HEADS

I've gathered you here, you three,
sitting before me just barely, with
stones upon your heads, and your friends
walk by, your nieces, put more
stones upon your heads. Do you remember
me? Dad, has the earth done things to
your brain so now you don't remember?
Mom? The earth has had you for so much
longer. And, Owen, I'm twelve years
older than you ever were. I want you
to know I'll never forget you, but I
can't go on writing poems about you.
I've discovered they don't bring
you back. They don't make me
understand you better. They don't
even win me prizes.

I live in a small town now. If you
came back, you'd never find me.
I sit on this bluff overlooking the lake
and count the birds against the sky.
The waves are grey and foamy creatures
that pounce for the rocks but just can't hold on.
I sit here. I write. I think about you
lying there. You picture me on a subway
or stuck in gridlock. But I'm here
in nature, with my little dog Lily,
and soon she and I
will gather some stones
to place upon your heads.

THE ROAD

The road is just a road.
No matter how
many hearses
stumble drunk
through its dirt
and pebbles; no
matter how many
birds fall dead
and raise dust;
no matter how
many buildings
collapse on either
side of it—the
road is just a road.
It did not ask to
be a road: it was
happy being
nothing.

GOES WITHOUT SAYING

allegretto pizzicato

GUESSWORK

after Charles North

This is a product.
I call it sunset farming.
Pigs will envelop you
in their illusory
command modules. I
shot a star across
the room and it landed
in chicken soup dribbling
off the roof
of a nine-storey apartment.
The horses devised
a quiz for me. I flunked.
I grew tentacles. It was
all guesswork.
          On reflection,
I would choose not to live
but simply to exist in a carport
in a bombed-out capital.
Charm and grace
get you the best
marks; next: a stiff
hairdo, your corpse's outline,
heel marks on linoleum.
I'm pretty downtown.
I live with ghosts.
Look at the frog
jump. It jumps
so easily.

FROM THE POETICS OF BECAUSE

after Mireia Calafell

The pail, the two speeches, a curve.
Loss is the culmination of the two because
ancient books descend from the corner
of an iron sculpture by Rodin:
a yak, a breathing compass,
a son, a "self-devourer"—all taunting the light.

Beds, sex, a caricature.
The keys to the jar of men
whose mouths go pow,
and block themselves from beer,
become an unsalted mess
while the deformed are formed
and water reaches its limit.

Mother with time, her eyes, the red calf.
We shall build ourselves Gutenbergs
as our ancestors did, without knowing our guts,
and sail into the focus of an excited fire,
raise purgatory from your coal
and wash—without actually washing—Paradise,
as our mirrors kiss ourselves.

MOVIE

after Eileen Myles

a tree
covered in fuzz
a volcano
to take to bed
and mimic
the way your shoulders
oval features
turning
too many embraces
through my teeth
your history
toward night
window open
calm gesture
the broken cup
at night
about your dog
very slowly
riddled with comments
doglike
fingers and toes
dark silence
flame far away
remain

PARC AVENUE, AUGUST 11, 2018, 10:18 AM

He wears shorts.
His shorts cough
around him. His legs,
sticks of wood
bursting with nails.
The vibration of
torn plastic sheeting.
She walks slowly
within a burqa.
She walks quickly
within a burqa.
He is crammed into
a dirty white smock.
Each hand clutches
a bag of onions.
From behind
a red baby carriage,
the reaching of a giraffe.
He trims leaves and smokes. A blue dress walks straight,
a woman inside it. An unlit cigarette stretches from her
lips. Within a black T-shirt, he kisses his dog, who is
outside the black T-shirt. And again. I walk straight on
slanted pavement. He kisses his dog. I react to nothing.
The onions do not react. A Zazers wrapper trembles in
the denuded flowerbox. Not enough cars to fill the road.
She carries a child. The
child's arm is extended,
pointed the way they
are walking. He wears
a red shirt. He carries
a blue bag in each
hand. Each bag
contains

bald plastic
heads. Honk.
The plastic heads
don't react. A
left hand is in
a pocket. A stroll
is present.
He kisses his big dog again. A happy lobster waves in
greeting. He wears a shtreimel. He wears a black coat. He
wears shiny black boots. Containeds. Strolleds. Walkeds.
Bounceds. Heards. Kisseds. Honk. Three women wear
black. Three women are the same height. Three women
walk at the same speed. My legs are unsteady.
I walk across
the crosswalk
slowly. He
coughs.

JOHN ASHBERY'S "THE PAINTER": DETAILS

Sitting
just silence
the sand, a brush

*

Until the end
angry
a prayer

*

How he them
not art?
forgetting the portrait

*

Slightly murmuring
the canvas building

*

even some buildings
sit for a portrait!

*

fade white
a howl
a prayer overcrowded

*

They the
And the
As though

24-HOUR CENTO

It is very early
I might get caught
I am weighed down with
the message of the night
These words were given to me to say:
guzzle, *flay* and *kablooey*
My head hurts, it is noon
Fog is polishing the street on its hands and knees.
I can barely be bothered to
dream.
Having no choice
the stars are singing to the stars.
Plash. Night. Plash. Sky.

NOW SHOWING

The crunch of popcorn faded.
The credits began rolling.
A rabbit chased an ostrich
in the open field.
They told me my name was Ed.
I threw a party
after my brother collapsed.
It was eleven forty-three.
Four wings were glued to my back.
Wonder all around me.
A boll weevil watched me from my untidy desk.
Beneath it I discovered
three sports cars and a duck.
I didn't know how to talk
as a result of phones hadn't yet been invented.
A window exploded.
Huge gusts of octopus
billowed out of my eyes.

THE TRAGICAL HISTORY OF THE LIFE AND DEATH OF DR. WALRUS

The walrus shovelled coal into the wood stove
The walrus shovelled dirt into the grave
The walrus shovelled mulch into its mouth
The walrus shovelled its way out of the avalanche
The walrus shovelled lies into its novel

For ten years I observed the walrus
For ten years I neglected my children's needs
For ten years clouds formed inside my brain
For ten years the banks cooked our dinners
For ten years television was banned

Who put gunpowder in the oatmeal?
Who put gunpowder on the dead priest's bedsheets?
Who put gunpowder behind that barely discernible planet?
Who put gunpowder in a barrel of gunpowder?
Who put gunpowder between the pages of this book?

SUSPICIONS

The concert contained music
which seated us in the front row.
Our stomachs rumbled, echoing
our suspicions. We remembered
when words were outlawed. They
put cheese in the maze. Detritus
was celebrating its birthday, and
the world gave it a marvellous
painting of a sofa. Have you ever
seen a wave walk across the
landscape of an ocean? A piece of
my life got jammed in some
rusted box springs. Today contains
as many minutes as yesterday, but
fewer frightened chickens. So
on moving day, we move on.
Meanwhile, something took place
at the same time. A person
told me heaven is nice. Life
was made up.

THE SCHOOLS SEEM PLEASED

after Ted Berrigan

I am too early.
The front of my brain
drank twice, became
a big hit in vaudeville.
Am I satisfied? Am
I a stalled car?
I have acquired skin,
which I wear close
to the editor of my bones.
In the middle
of exhaustion, the schools
seem pleased. They grin,
they hammer the great
American themes. They drink.
The airlines drink. The
chapel drinks of its own
fragrance. We call this
rock and roll.
                    I turn on
Prague, but turn off Poland.
The bus stops with a grunt.
"Come home," it rasps. A gift
is tied with a ribbon. A scarecrow
is tied with a telephone wire.
When I wake up, I am the size
of an aspirin. My injuries
are broadcast on TV. Demonstrations
gather in the square, filled with
the children who have emerged
from the corners of curious
objects. "We have something
to tell you, Hart Crane."

MORTALITY CENTO

Can you hear me?
The road to death
where there is no time
is invisible,
I peep into the hole
I remember buying headless smelts
I am told I am not bad looking
I can draw power
without interrupting your sleep!
When we say something is beautiful
The rat says, "God, I *hate* irony."

LADIES & GENTLEMEN, THE SOLAR SYSTEM

Holy the monster that ricocheted off the spongy
stars. Ugly astronaut without oxygen tank drifted
amid the planets.

I left my wallet at home. I patted my empty pockets.
I would be arrested for theft, the police were tireless.
Then, in an alley I found cash. Soon everything would
be different. I experienced equal parts fear and regret.

The trees knew, and the birds.

A contorted face peered over the brick wall surrounding
the crumbling Safeway filled with shoppers, shirts torn
and stained by mustard. Mr. Nightingale, watching
from a van, recognized the face immediately. It was she
who...she who...He was transported back to Grade 2
phys. ed., and a deft kick in the ribs.

The trees knew, and the birds, that my liver lived in
another man. They stared into the night sky, stretching
their branches and wing tips as far as they could
manage. The moon glistened on their foreheads.

One by one, each man and woman stepped forward and
threw a handful of dirt on the coffin.

The mammal was of indeterminate temperament.
Paparazzi followed it everywhere, flashbulbs exploding. It
was all over the newspapers. People spoke of nothing else.

My pockets were filled with money now, pockets that
had been empty for so long. My eyes bulged—there were
stores everywhere.

A year later, she placed a small rock on top of the headstone. It was something Jews did. She had never asked him, and now it was too late.

A page filled with instructions in an unknown alphabet floated by. The astronaut reached for it and missed.

The trees knew, and the birds, the leaves and the feathers. The planets knew, and the sun, the stars, the space junk. The reflection in a bedroom window of a woman with her face in her hands.

Soon everything would be different. The doors in the hotel lobby locked automatically and the guests backed away, toward the elevators. The PA system crackled, voiceless. The elevators remained stationary. A man hooked up to an IV reached into his pocket, took out a paperback, began reading aloud.

The citizens badmouthed the city. Where had they found the courage? We swayed beneath the impermeable armour of the polite clouds. Echoes scraped across all surfaces. Then: rain. Then: locusts. The death of the first-born. Someone had a great idea for a TV show.

IMPORTANT INFORMATION FOR YOUR DENTAL HEALTH

I have never had a root canal, but
my friend Mary just had one and
she is lying in bed all weekend because
apparently they are very painful. I
wrote and told her I have never had
a root canal and I hope I never have
one, but now all I can think about
is that it is inevitable, someday I will
have a root canal, even though my
teeth are pretty good; my dentist
Rick Cameron is always surprised when
I skip three years of appointments and
I still don't have any cavities and none
of my teeth have fallen out, I'm pretty
lucky that way. My mother had really
good teeth and she always used to
clean between them with the corners
of business cards, her teeth were
always so white. They clicked like
mah jong tiles. The best way
to avoid a root canal is to replace
your head with a sparrow.

STATIC IS TERRIBLE

after "Tragg's Choice 2" by Clint Burnham

Something magical occurs
To capture me
All the crinkled
Talking to my own smashed radio
I don't know why
Careen from the clouds
It happens
Slipping up from the earth
To capture me
Each time I close my eyes
Rinsing the ideas from my head
Right at the moment that
Inky patches form on my arms
Black snowflakes that
Leave my skin full of words
Eat tiny tunnels through my skull

GOES WITHOUT SAYING

after Maxine Chernoff's "Granted"

The mug atop your neck, I noticed,
approached my nose-holder, and wet flakes sailed
into the security mechanism and out the other side,
unclosing the knobbed rectangle.
You and I entered and gazed upon
transparent panes the colours of grass and sponge toffee.
The April–June season was harsher than
December–March, whose *Lobularia maritime*
and *Trifolium*, teamed with the very burden
of breathing oxygen, drove us beyond
the word repository. In our sleep vessel we remained
for twelve-month stretches, and, unrushed,
ingested health-restoration devices
from one another's drinking vessels.
We devoured Charles Dickens
and kept our greenbacks
in our stockings.
Not a thing unclosed while
we undertook this.

INCIDENT REPORT

12:23 p.m.—Hank stares at an inkblot test.

12:23 p.m.—A severed foot washes up in Kitsilano.

12:23 p.m.—Misty googles "do mice have thoraxes?"

12:23 p.m. —Two passing bus drivers wave.

12:23 p.m.—A boy scares another boy: turns his eyelids
inside out.

12:23 p.m.—Her breathing stops as his fingers touch her
cheek.

12:23 p.m.—Raindrops on the sidewalks of Burlington.

12:23 p.m.—A great silence descends in kindergarten
class.

12:23 p.m.—Peppy's owner throws her half an almond.

12:23 p.m.—A kettle (whose owner is dead) whistles.
A requiem.

ZIGZAG (Poem for January 1, 2017)

Yesterday the newspaper said one thing;
today it says something entirely different.
And all we did to make that happen
was sleep. Today I looked in the mirror,
and *I* was unrecognizable! A meadowlark
with a broken wing. The news
is printed on paper while the meadow
is printed on lark, and we focus
our camera (a Filmo Sportster
manufactured 1947 by Bell & Howell)
on it as it zigzags into the air,
carrying just one thing under its bum wing:
a copy of *Company*, by Samuel Beckett
(published 1979 by John Calder). The pollsters
find that people want to hear seven words
from *Company*. The meadowlark, although
struggling to remain in flight, complies:
"girdle," "inkling," "confusion," "vertex,"
"mountains," "hitherto," and "furthermore."
Seven words of inspiration! Today
the people are frightened but
tomorrow they will rise up. Imagine
what might be possible! In 1702, when
this poem was written, the author
was put to death: an enemy of the state.
In crafting this translation, I have
striven to maintain the vitality
of the original. In this way, the frightened
people will rise up, probably tomorrow.
Imagine what might be possible!

APHRODITTY

I open my mouth and let the world
mouth, I will not bathe it and
animal, tree, and Lily lies at my you
say I should place a penny and I
put a penny on my tongue who
sleep in the streets, but of a
penny on my tongue but I don't
need to worry about feeding
sleeping and she doesn't know
what and so I will not eat a
penny unaware of capitalism and
poverty juice but I will put
this poem lying in an empty
doorway my cradle the love
of Lily on my tongue I will
not put a penny in my in, the
breaths of every person, my
tongue in orange juice, and
feet, she always lies at my
feet, on my head and parade
by those, my tongue recoils at
the thought their dogs still love
them and I Lily doesn't recoil
because she is my dog before I
feed myself a penny is anyway,
is totally nor drink the sugar
of orange and I could just as
easily be upon my head and I
will body curled against Lily,
and really

WHATEVER YOU DESIRE

allegro molto

HE: A POETICS

He put doughnuts on the table, a box
of them. He was making some point.
"You are all doughnuts in a box."
"If you could choose only one
doughnut..." "Why do doughnuts
have holes in them?" I don't remember
his point, but he was making a point
in the name of team-building. We all
hated him. He could not buy us off
with doughnuts or with philosophy
built around the existential hole
in the middle of a doughnut. He
hated us too. I want to phone him up,
wherever he is now, and tell him
his fucking doughnuts make no
impression on me beyond the fact
that he put a box of them on the table.
I hope he has failed in everything
in his life. I hope he is estranged
from his family. I hope he is
walking up and down the subway
cars, holding out boxes of doughnuts
to people who don't give a shit
what his doughnuts mean. I hope
his faith in capitalism has collapsed.
I am walking my dog. Because it is
21 degrees below 0 (Celsius) and
because it has snowed and the
people of my little town have
dumped salt on the sidewalks
even though there are more dogs
in this town than there are humans,
I have put little red rubber boots
on my dog. The name of my dog

is Lily. We found her at a rescue
in Cornwall, Ontario, near the Quebec
border. They called her Lily there
even though her papers say her
name is Croquette. (She is of French-
Canadian origin.) The heater
in my car isn't working. I just
get cold air when I turn it on.
It is very hard to make friends
in a small town. There are eight
pizza places here but there is no
Indian food. Like me, Lily
doesn't like doughnuts or the
lessons they might teach us.
A lot of poets think it is
important to write poems that
are about "issues." They judge
poems by the stance the poem
takes on issues. Lily and I decide
whether we like a poem just by its tone
and the words it uses, the images,
the juxtapositions; we don't really
care what the poem "means."
If Lily doesn't wear those little
red rubber boots (they're actually
more like tiny balloons) then she
will walk for a bit and suddenly she
will lift a paw and look at me with
this helpless look. She will walk on
only three paws. I pick her up and
gather her into the warmth of my
jacket-covered arms and I pull her
close to my body. Things have really
changed since I was a child. Back then,
dogs roamed free. When they'd been
out for a while, you'd open your door

and you'd call them. Soon they would
arrive on the porch. They would put
down their little briefcases and fold
their glasses into their glasses case.
Back then, there was only one kind
of doughnut. Oscar Williams edited
all the poetry anthologies. You would watch
the black-and-white TV from a motel room
and see a man jump around on the moon.
Every good poem, according to Lily,
ends with the word "moon."

THE FOOD COURT

You could get anything down there in the Food Court: egg rolls and chicken balls, spaghetti, banquet burgers, pizza with pepperoni, tuna sandwiches, souvlaki. It was like you had the whole world at your fingertips, my dad used to say. You could travel from continent to continent without ever getting on a plane. So Murray and Ken went down the escalator first, because I was moving slower, since my arms were full. I was still near the top when they reached the bottom and I saw them step out into the Food Court and look around, their eyes wide. On the escalator, which was moving stairs, you could just stand there, not moving your feet, and then you would be downstairs. But I guess the problem was I was a bit impatient, eager to catch up to Murray and Ken, and I took a few steps down and stumbled a bit, and I dropped everything. I watched it all bounce down the moving stairs of the escalator: my book bag, my records, and my dad's wooden coffin. Murray and Ken heard the racket, and saw all that stuff coming down, and me regaining my balance and running after it. The people in the up escalator stared at me as they went past. When I caught up, Murray and Ken each had one end of my dad's coffin. They flipped it; it had landed upside down. "I always drop that," I told them. Murray put my records and my book bag on top of the pine box, and we wandered from one food booth to the next. Ken got a tuna sandwich, Murray got souvlaki, and I got spaghetti, which was also my dad's favourite, which was probably why I got it. I showed them my records while we ate, and Murray grabbed the Linda Ronstadt one from my hands and looked at the cover, where she was sitting on a bale of hay with her guitar and wearing a bonnet. "She's so beautiful," Murray said. "I hope I get a girl like that."

MY BOSS

My boss was a blend of miniature schnauzer and bichon frise. My boss treated me well. Gave me treats. I married my boss's daughter. My boss offered six months' mat leave when we had twins (one two-legged, one four-legged). My boss was loyal. My boss sat and rolled over and offered a paw. I took my boss for walks. We walked to parks and down by the lake. My boss threatened to fire me when I said bad things about fire hydrants. When I balked at presenting my rear for a sniff. I gave my boss 100 per cent. I would do anything for my boss. I chased my boss when my boss chased kids on skateboards. My boss suggested I get a tattoo of my boss on my left forearm. This I did. Others also worked for my boss. I did not know their names. My boss asked what breed I was. My boss did not like being patted on the head but took pleasure from being scratched under the chin. This was not part of my job description. I did it anyway. When we were walking, people would ask what kind of boss that was. They would say, "It's obvious who is the boss."

EL HINDU

I had a bunch of papers to copy. Stories I wrote about
things in my life were what those papers consisted of. I
went to El Hindu because that place had a copier machine
in addition to books and various stationery products. A
man was crying behind the counter. He was the owner,
and he was the only one allowed to operate the machine.
His white shirt was neatly pressed. His scarred hands
were flat on the counter before him. I offered him a
slice of apple, because its coolness and freshness would
comfort him. I had seventy-four sheets of paper to copy.
But the man was upset, and I didn't want to bother him
with matters of business. My career as a writer could wait,
just as it had waited all my life until now. His tears were
gathering in his bushy moustache. Outside, the sun was
sinking behind the Plaza of the Congress. The electric
light in El Hindu made a buzzing sound and flickered.
The man looked at me; his eyes were red and glazed. I
riffled the edge of my stack of papers I needed to copy. A
television was on but the sound was off. People's mouths
moved but they said nothing. I was particularly nervous.

THE FIRST TETRAPODS

for Heather Hogan

Rib Fest provided us with great
opportunities, in particular to eat
ribs out of the sides of cows, their
juices dribbling into the grasses
of Victoria Park. But when I arrived
there were no ribs left, all the ribs
were gone, but there was a little
cole slaw and a forest of trophies
for Best Ribs, Juiciest Ribs, Most
Intellectual Ribs, Spiciest Ribs,
Most Shapely Ribs, Tangiest
Ribs, Most Tender Ribs, Ribs
With Most Tendons, Happiest
Ribs. Now here is the remarkable
thing: the cows were content. Rib-
less, their torsos collapsing, they
grazed by the bandshell,
listening to songs by Charley Pride.
"The first tetrapods were aquatic,"
Heather explained to me. She was
an estate lawyer with a certain
flair who had once flown to
Istanbul for work. I made a joke
about "Phoenician blinds." The
rib chefs took down their booths.
They were wracked with pride.
I forget what happened next.

VARIOUS RECORDS
(Poem for January 1, 2018)

Open one eye and then the other. But when you open
the second one, close the first one. This way,
you give each eye its day in the sun. The sun glints
off the desert of snow that covers your driveway.
The streets are empty. Your favourite record
is playing in the sky. Wisps of clouds occasionally
muffle the sound. This is the first day.
One of your eyes, maybe your left, goes out
to shovel, while the other, likely your right,
stays in and makes breakfast. Butter smeared
on a dark rye plus genmai tea, with pieces of walnut
floating on top. Right now, the catastrophe seems
very far away. Your phone rings. Someone wants
to talk with you about a particular page in a book
you either wrote or read: the connection is bad.
But all words are good, it doesn't matter what
anyone says, so long as they say it, and you hear
something. Let one ear listen and then the other.
It is true that there are people you once knew
who are no longer alive. It doesn't mean you can't
hug them or tell them about a painting you saw
or laugh at their jokes. One of the jokes hinges
on "bird's eye view" vs. "birds I view." And by now
your impeccable driveway is flanked by huge
berms of snow and you are using a spoon to get
at the last few walnut pieces from the bottom
of your mug. You are only one person. The earth
is covered in individuals. Various records
play in the sky.

RON PADGETT'S POEM "JUNE 17, 1942"

I am listening to Ron Padgett and he is twenty-eight years old.
"June 17, 1942" is way heavier when I hear Ron's young voice
reciting it than when I read it on the page in *Toujours L'Amour*.
Was he really that mean to his grandparents? Was his mother
really the saddest person on earth? Outside it is raining.
The moon ripples behind smudged clouds as if the real world
were an old horror movie starring Lon Chaney Jr. The first time
I saw the actual Ron Padgett was in the Art Institute of Chicago.
He was walking along beside Anselm Hollo. How tall he was.
Like a giraffe with two t's running off the end of his name
like the two f's in giraffe which he said are like two giraffes
running through the word *giraffe*. I saw Ron again
twenty minutes later when we crossed paths again in another
room in the gallery. I don't remember what the art was
but it was probably contemporary, maybe some Jim Dine,
some Yoko Ono, because I don't like much of the old stuff,
and then, one more time I passed Ron and his friend
Anselm in yet another room and I heard him speak.
That warm voice coming from his bespectacled tallness
reassured me that this was the world I had chosen,
poets weaving in and out of galleries, twenty-four hours a day.
And later, I saw him and Anselm Hollo read at the School
of the Art Institute of Chicago. After, my friend Richard Huttel
took a photo of Ron with his arm around my shoulder when I
finally introduced myself to him: "I'm the guy who sent you
that chapbook, *Ladies & Gentlemen, Mr. Ron Padgett*" (which I didn't
actually say but look how it adds dramatic effect to this poem).

An arm of Ron Padgett was around my shoulder!

And now Ron is old and I am close to old, though already old
to the young poets who have no interest in me, and Ron
is doing something right now. Anything that Ron does
is interesting, in my opinion, so he is doing something

interesting now in New York City, where he lives. Now when
I'm writing this and now when you're reading this. Maybe
he is listening to his twenty-eight-year-old self read
"June 17, 1942" (the day he was born), but I doubt it. Maybe
he is sitting in the Neptune Diner eating a bowl of matzoh-
ball soup and thinking about some untranslated poem by
Guillaume Apollinaire. I am listening to the sound of
car tires rolling up and down Division Street in Cobourg,
where I live, and you can tell the streets are slushy with
snow and rain from how that sound sounds. I have never
stopped to think about the word *household*. A household
is comprised of all the members of the family who live
in the house, plus the servants. I summon one of my servants.
He tells me he has never stopped to think about the word
summon. "I bet summon wants to me to go fetch a book
by Ron Padgett," he says. I ask for *Triangles in the Afternoon*,
which is located in my piano bench.

Now here is the strange thing:

I just researched triangles and discovered that the triangle
falls into a class of musical instruments known as idiophones.
Yesterday in Toronto I bought the book *Idiophone* by Amy
Fusselman. I didn't know what an idiophone was
but I bought it anyway because I really liked her books
8 and *The Pharmacist's Mate*. The first line of Amy Fusselman's
book *Idiophone* is "I can't sleep in this uncomfortable
New York City cab." Once in New York City I was with
Ron Padgett and we saw his friend Richard Hell.
Name-dropping is the best way to end any poem. Name-
dropping is the best way to end any poem.

LOVE IS, DOT DOT DOT

Because John's mother expressed an interest
in knitting didn't mean John had to be
a tapestry himself. He jimmied
open her diary and discovered his father
was a turtle in a cable-knit sweater
and Jesus was his boss. While he
buried the book in her garden,
he saw the tulips were covered
in jelly. He ran away from home and
tried to lose himself among the parishioners.
When the sun fell, he constructed
a bus station out of various
scraps of this and that drifting
along the street, bought a ticket
and disappeared down the highway,
nodding off against the window.
How many towns did John
pass through before he disembarked?
He settled in a place called Elbow
where everyone was a crook.

His mother turned pale and
died beneath a tattered quilt.
No one had held her hand.
She was buried in her garden,
where she found her own secrets.
When people died, it turned out,
they kept thinking. This was
a grand surprise. The parishioners
were intimate with their livestock.
John became the mayor
of Elbow, where he
instituted several positive
changes.

POEM BEGINNING WITH A LINE BY DEAN YOUNG

Because I will die soon, I fall asleep
and while I sleep, I count the days
in which I saw you. And of these days,
I count the days we were in love.
Someone has left the window open, it's
not their fault, they didn't know
it would rain, and the drops soon
turn dark the sheet that covers me
to my shoulders. You have told me
it's okay to leave you behind, I
shouldn't feel guilt, and also
you will be okay and use all
your freed-up time to paint
the lake every seven days or
every ten. The colour is never
the same. The number of birds
is always changing. The sun's
reflection is differently misshaped.
And I will become earth
and you will make toast and
walk the dog that looks
for me every day.

IRONING

It was while he was plugging in the iron that it struck him. Not the iron but the realization. He knew something had felt different—for weeks, maybe even months. The pressure of the air against his skin, the feel of the breeze through his thinning hair, the decreasing grip of his feet against the floor. He was, he saw now, being shed. Had he plugged in the iron—or even just stopped to think—a few weeks earlier, he might have known then. Maybe he could have done something then. Maybe he could have reversed the process. Too late now. He placed the hot iron on the stove so as not to ruin any surfaces, and packed a few of his things. It was dark still so early in the morning, but he knew the way to the woods. He lay on his back just off a path that he hiked nearly every day and placed a large rock on his belly. Soon he would be little more than a translucent piece of onion paper, his name typed unevenly on it with an Olympia manual typewriter. The wind was picking up now. He didn't want to blow away.

WHATEVER YOU DESIRE

Look at the tree burst from the top of my skull so recently mown as my friends disappear Look at my car losing control and sliding off the road into the snowy ravine as my friends disappear Look at the drunken sky pressing its ugly belly into the fragile mountains about to collapse as my friends disappear Look at the fine zigzag cracks forming at my ankles and spreading toward my groin as my friends disappear Look at Saul Bass's credits for *Vertigo* as my friends disappear Look at the rabbits cowering in the closet of the Motor Vehicle Registration Office as outside the air becomes filled with balloons as my friends disappear Look at the blood leaking from this plate of vegetables as my friends disappear Look at my father phoning me once again from the dead he forgot to mention that he buried all the Monopoly pieces in a Seagram's bag in the backyard on Pannahill as my friends disappear Look at my friends the backs of their heads their brains pushing out of their ears again their legs moving like mechanical stilts their words spilling from their mouths like blinking neon lights as my friends disappear Look at the remains of the soldier I pretended to kill in the staircase of my high school in 1974 Look at the door lying in the centre of the lawn and imagine what would happen if you opened it Look at my grandmother's Russian accent look how she fries up the chicken fat look at her putting my grandfather's dinner on the tray in front of him as my friends disappear Look at the crane in the distance smell the gasoline as you stand in front of your brother's grave Look at the frightened boll weevil Look at the cartoon penguin on the TV as mother lies in a coma as my friends disappear Look at the clock look at the tangled hair in the comb look at the oil the car left on the road and how it glistens and takes on the shape of whatever you desire

126

DREAM ANALYSIS II

A small grey rat
peered across
my patio at me.
He came closer
and closer
until his snout
was almost in my face.
He was enormous,
his nose twitched.
He would engulf me.
This was a dream.

In dreams, the rat, or any rodent, symbolizes the unrelenting, brutal power of the military. A patio represents vulnerability, the rawness of your being. In this way, you are trampled, bulldozed, by the approach of lumbering tanks. The snout represents indecision, while the human face is a symbol of doubt and, occasionally, hopelessness. After bearing your soul and having it crushed, you are confronted by indecision meeting hopelessness. The sensation of being engulfed is the return to the womb. In this way, the rat has exposed you and sent you scurrying back to a state before your birth.

THRIFTY AND SCALY

My mother asks me what is in my duffel bag. "My lunch," I say. "I mean, my gym equipment." There is no way I am paying $28 to see some fish. To get into the aquarium for free, you sneak around to the rear loading docks, unzip your duffel bag, and remove your giant trout outfit. Making sure no one is watching, you strip down and step into the trout. Throwing yourself to the ground, you shout, "There's a big trout out here—help! It's dying," and you thrash about, whipping your tail and head violently until the metal door swings open, and Sarah and Severino, the aquarium interns, lift you and carry you to the safety of your tank.

TORONTO

They all lived on Queen Street they
wrote novels about living on Queen
Street they wrote novels about
writing a novel on Queen Street they
all appeared in each other's novels
there was this one bartender there
was this one musician there was
this one girl from camh she smoked
du maurier cigarettes everyone
looked into the sky the clouds were
sort of weird a bat sailed above
the telephone wires and swooped
behind a warehouse taxi cabs
whipped back and forth Depeche
Mode leaked out from a bar a kid
wearing a Keep On Truckin' tee
pulled a red wagon along the
sidewalk in the wagon was
the actual Queen of England her
name was Elizabeth Two behind
her her corgis trotted along
barking at inanimate objects
when the people of Queen Street
realized who was among them
they sewed together fig leaves
and made they for themselves
aprons of modest splendour

REGARDING MY GREATEST WORK

I have often been asked, in circumstances similar to these, as I stood before an auditorium whose benches overflowed with enthusiastic listeners just like you, and upon whose rafters perched still more, how I came to write my greatest work, "The Arc of the Pontoon." My arms extend from my shoulders like vacuum cleaner hoses, and I hold them like so, with my hands palm-up, as if to say, *I take you all in, I welcome each of you into my world, come unto me.* In this way, I draw you into my dust basket using my tremendous suction powers. It is not, you see, enough to simply be a good writer; you must also have impressive and unpredictable suction capabilities. I wrote "The Arc of the Pontoon" twenty-seven years ago, when my name was barely known in poetry circles. I had no idea my work would arrive like an earthquake rattling the literary community of our country (and, in translation, those of countries beyond our borders). From your position crouched snugly within my dust basket, you can imagine me lying in bed, in winter, beneath thick blankets. The voice of my mother comes from downstairs: it is 6:30 and I must open the gas station at 7:15. The pump, too, has a hose attached to its body—the *bensinslange*, our Norwegian friends call it. I drag myself from beneath the covers, pull on my bathrobe, and plod down the carpeted stairs. Still largely asleep, I navigate my way to the kitchen, where my mother is putting my luncheon meat sandwiches in resealable plastic bags, and I say to her, without even thinking, "The arc of the pontoon is the conscience of our people." Both my mother and I are startled. That sentence contains no fewer than three words I have never before uttered aloud. You can imagine how things proceeded after that, the irresistible momentum that carried me from that moment until this. And it is inarguable that rigorous testing has established beyond question that vacuuming can kill 100 per cent of infant fleas and as many as 96 per cent of adult fleas.

THE CROWD

There was an explosion of heat and then wind blew hard
through his wiry hair. When he opened his eyes he saw
that he stood at the base of a ladder. He began to climb.
Soon, on reaching one hand up, he felt something soft,
something giving. It was like a bellows, or perhaps a
stomach. As he climbed, it gave way, and he found himself
inside it. A small seat moulded itself around his thighs
and buttocks as he settled into it. Now he wondered who
he was. Now the walls of the chamber pressed against him.
His breathing, necessarily, became shallow. Who was this
person in whose body he found himself? No, that wasn't
right. Whose was this mind suspended in the skull of his
body? Something glowed in front of him. He reached
forward until his fingertips touched a pale screen. Where
he made contact, images began to flow. Shadows gave way
to landscapes, then to structures, then to smaller figures,
figures he soon recognized as people. Several women
stood on a makeshift stage. They moved in staccato,
from one part of the stage to another. He recoiled as the
face of one woman filled the screen. He could see the
striations in her lips, the fine hairs in her nostrils, the
blood vessels on the sclera of her eyes. He touched his
own lips, skimmed his nostrils, brushed the surface of his
eyes. There was a spark of recognition, which he trapped
within his hand before it became extinguished. Now the
screen went dark and sank back into the soft wall, and
he peered down at his closed fist. The faintest glimmer
showed between his fingers. He grasped the next rung of
the ladder and pulled himself to his feet, began climbing
again. He emerged from the top of the chamber and cool
air flowed past his cheeks like a stream. He opened his
closed fist, and all that he had done, everything he had
built and created and decided and achieved and failed
at, all of it drifted into the air, became windborne. Now

he was separated from his own actions. Now he felt a lightness. Some time passed: he could feel it through his thinning hair. An expansiveness formed in his chest and propelled him. Now he was moving through scenery: buildings, mailboxes, trees, fire hydrants, riverbeds. He rolled down the window and watched carefully. A light changed from one colour to another colour, and a mass of people began to surge forward. He looked for himself among them.

MOTEL OF THE OPPOSABLE THUMBS

in memory of Sydney Ross

We soar through the night. Bugs spatter our windshield.
My father, he's alive again. Steers with one hand.
Our headlights bounce the road. Air whips our hair.

He sucks on smoke. I clutch a bag of chips.
The moon sucks on clouds. A bat flits by.
My father flicks on the radio. The highway spasms.

A dark rectangle. VACANCY ruptures the horizon.
"We'll stop here." My father's deep rumble.
I'm nearing sixty. He is long dead.

He sits on the edge of his twin bed. I sit on mine.
Mould in the bathroom. A spider on the lampshade.
"And the nurse slid the ring from my still, withered

hand and handed it to you in the corridor." Light sputters.
The Coke machine rattles. I slide under the covers.
The highway goes silent. I can't warm my hands.

SUBTITLES

I wake up. A truck stutters by
on the road outside last year's
window. Its rumble fades to a wisp.
This year I will make a grilled
cheese sandwich with tomato.
I make it. I put it on a plate.
The plate is cracked. The kitchen
light flickers. The phone almost
rings. Protestors chant outside
my door. I step out onto the porch,
lift a megaphone to my lips. Aloft
I hold the grilled cheese sandwich.
I request the protestors' silence.
Their din curls into a tiny ball,
rolls down the street and off
the pier, drops into the happy lake.
I am about to speak, forming
words in my head like *beseech* and *implore*,
verisimilitude and *providence*, when
2019 reaches over the horizon,
hurling its vast shadow over us.
A song pops into my head. I record it.
It becomes the latest craze. Protestors
dance to it. Citizens plan their year
around it. It is called "Chekhov Said
If You Introduce a Grilled Cheese Sandwich
in Act One, You Must Shoot Someone
With It in Act Three." But it is just a thing
I wrote. I didn't mean anything by it.
I look for my little white dog
in the clouds but it's like trying
to read subtitles against snow.
Did I tell you about the time
my mother hunched over my

fever-dampened brow? She
drew the blankets to my pale neck
and murmured to me,
You will spend the rest of your life
trying to remember
what I murmured to you.

1 January 2019

NOTES ON THE CONTRIBUTORS

Florence Kneepoliti is the author of *Filthcap*. Born in Ljubljana, Missouri, she teaches in the Humanities Department of Tom Sawyer & Friends College. **Cheree R. Muckus** placed second in the Crad Flowers Sestina Competition. She collects bees and works as a lyric poetry counsellor at Placemat Forest Serviette in Crumbling Balcony, Saskatchewan. **Zachary Plop-Fitzhenrick** is the Fiona Ashbery Chair in Postmodernishism at University of Pompano Beach at Buffalo. **People Goldberg** are the author of three collections, most recently *Carbohydration Nerve Ending*. They live in Dog Trainer, North Carolina. **Billi Seventy-Nine** sells insurance in Norwegia, New Zealand. "I Sell Insurance" is his first published poem. **Sara(h) Tiny** won the Jo(h)n Tiny Pre-Memorial Prize for *Sonnet Preponderance Trilogy*. She teaches hypermodernesque poetics to pharmacology students at Puckering College in scenic Trondheim, Fisticuffs. **Suratt Sors** assembles cartoon ducks at Jimmies Carter & Durante Polytechnic. "Ezra Pound and I" is the only poem he ever wrote. **H. Body Kaplonsky** was Dean of Opal Louis Nations College for three decades. His seventeenth verse collection, *7/teen*, will be published posthumously next year. **Gillian Popa** is a constant cloud rider at Carla Porridge House in Canada, America. This is her third appearance in *Opposable*.

NOTES & ACKNOWLEDGEMENTS

"Considerably Sarah," for Sarah Burgoyne, borrows from her work, and appeared in *S=A=R=A=H B=U=R=G=O=Y=N=E = IN TRANSLATION =* (Montreal: Godwitch Hall Press, 2018). Thanks to Paige Cooper and Hilary Bergen.

"My Boss" appeared in the pocket zine *dog* (Missoula, Montana: Slumgullion Press, 2017). Thanks to debby florence.

"A Dog" appeared in *illiterature*. Thanks to Michael e. Casteels.

"The Open Window" and "Various Records (Poem for January 1, 2018)" appeared in *Spoon River Poetry Review*. Thanks to Kirstin Hotelling Zona.

"Sunrise with Sea Monsters" appeared on Paul Vermeersch's blog of the same name. Thanks, Paul.

"Ladies & Gentlemen, the Solar System" was a chapbook from Proper Tales Press.

"3" appeared on *dusie* (thanks to rob mclennan) and as a leaflet from Proper Tales Press.

"Thrifty and Scaly," "The First Tetrapods," and "Toronto" appeared on *Echolocation*. Thanks to Emily Iszak & Co.

"Occasional Poem" appeared in *Moebius*, translated into French as "Poème Occasionnel" by Catherine Cormier-Larose. Merci, Catherine.

"The Phil Halls" appeared on Newpoetry.ca. Thanks to George Murray.

"Grey Snotes" was a Proper Tales Press chapbook.

"Birthday" and "At Laundromats Here There Are No Dryers" appeared on *Rusty Toque*. Thanks, Kathryn Mockler.

"Rain," "Movie," and "Birthday" appeared as the trifold leaflet *Rain Movie Birthday* from Happy Monks Press in Wilmington, North Carolina. Thanks to Alessandro Porco.

"Please Write This Down" was written while listening to Barbara Guest's "The Türler Lenses."

"Guesswork" was written while listening to Charles North's "Building Sixteens." It is essential that you read Charles North.

"Conniption Sauce" was written while listening to John Ashbery's *Flow Chart*.

"The Arrival of My Grandfather from Russia" was written while listening to Louise Glück's "Faithful and Virtuous Night."

"Aphroditty" and "Parc Avenue, August 11, 2018, 10:18 AM" were written in Montreal in August 2018 in Sarah Burgoyne's excellent workshop Tentacular Thinking and Writing.

"From the Poetics of Because" is a faux translation, from the Catalan, of a poem from *Poètiques del cos*, by Mireia Calafell.

"Broken Spoke" consists of three poems written between the lines of Mary Ruefle's poem of the same name.

"Motel Poem" ends with a sentence from the journal of Sir Robert Falcon Scott.

"Considerably Sarah" is for Sarah Burgoyne on her thirtieth birthday. "Fifty Words for Gwen, Plus a Title" is for Gwendolyn Guth on her fiftieth birthday. "You Step Out onto Your Porch" is for Michael Dennis on his sixtieth birthday.

"Poetry or Baseball" is for George Bowering and Jean Baird.

"Nancy" is comprised of lines from Ernest Bushmiller's comic strip *Nancy*, from which Joe Brainard drew inspiration.

"The Road" begins with a line by Paul Hoover.

"Notley 1" was meant to be a series of poems somehow based on texts by Alice Notley. I have no memory of how I constructed it, and so I cannot write "Notley 2."

"Alterations" borrows from Paul Éluard's "Love Again" ("O closed heart O heavy heart O deep heart / You will never get used to sorrow") and Roberto Bolaño's "The King of Parks" ("What's a guy like you doing here? / Are you plotting a crime?"

*

Thanks for the valuable feedback on various of these poems, especially to Laurie Siblock and Dag T. Straumsvåg, but also to Sarah Moses, Jaime Forsythe, and Steve Venright.

Thanks for the thoughtful marathon discussion on the concept of this book, Alessandro Porco.

Thanks to Brian Kaufman, Karen Green, and the whole Anvil crew for their faith in my work, plus Clint Hutzulak of Rayola.com and artist Stephen Lack for the cover.

Thanks to Lynn Crosbie and "Nashville" Jim Moran for their empathy and love in helping me through the last days of darling Lily; that's an important part of this book.

Thanks once more to Laurie Siblock, this time for more than I can articulate.

The extraordinary Larry Fagin provided mind-altering input for some of these poems; I learned so much from him. Please read his poems.

Since my last collection was published, we've lost seven poets whose works of extraordinary intelligence and beauty were central to me. Good night, John Ashbery, Bill Berkson, Tom Clark, Larry Fagin, Richard Huttel, David W. McFadden, Joe Rosenblatt.

Support from the residents of Ontario through the Ontario Arts Council's Works in Progress and Writers' Reserve programs bought me the time I needed to complete this manuscript.

I am grateful to my Patreon supporters, whose generosity gives me additional space to work on my various literary projects. Visit patreon.com/stuartross.

This book is loosely structured after Bela Bartók's String Quartet #4. I think I was only kidding about that when I included it in my notes for the sales force and promptly forgot I'd ever said it. Then it started appearing in online descriptions of this book and I figured I'd better give it a go. I hope someday to structure a book after Slothrust's 2014 album *Of Course You Do* and another after Nick Lowe's haircut.

For God's sake look after our people.

ABOUT THE AUTHOR

Stuart Ross is a writer, editor, writing teacher, and small press activist living in Cobourg, Ontario. He got his start selling his self-published chapbooks on the streets of Toronto and is now the prize-winning author of more than twenty books of poetry, fiction, and essays, most recently the poetry collection *A Sparrow Came Down Resplendent* (Wolsak and Wynn, 2016) and the novel in prose poems, *Pockets* (ECW Press, 2017). Stuart has given readings and taught writing workshops across the country and beyond. He was the 2010 Writer-in-Residence at Queen's University and has won the ReLit Award for Short Fiction, the Elaine Mona Adilman Award for Fiction on a Jewish Theme, the Canadian Jewish Literary Award for Poetry, the Battle of the Bards, the award for best Anglo book from l'Académie de la vie littéraire, and the Kitty Lewis Hazel Millar Dennis Tourbin Poetry Prize from Today's Book of Poetry. Stuart recently appeared at the Toronto International Festival of Authors and the Vilenica International Literary Festival in Slovenia. His poems have been translated into French, Spanish, German, Nynorsk, Russian, and Slovenian. He is currently working on a dozen different poetry, non-fiction, and fiction manuscripts.